Newgate—G...

by A.D. Walton

Published by Newcastle Libraries
& Information Service

Front cover:
The original 'Big Lamp' which gave its
name to the area, as seen from
Summerhill Street. Behind the 1890s
horse tram in Westgate Road is the
cholera epidemic burial ground. The
Tindal Street houses behind once led to
the Gem cinema in an adapted chapel.

Acknowledgements:

The photographs in this book are
reproduced by kind permission of the
following:

Newcastle City Libraries & Arts: cover, 1,
5, 6, 10, 15, 16, 17, 18, 21
West Newcastle Local Studies: 2, 9, 11,
12, 14, 19, 20
WNLS / K. Denholm: 3
WNLS / Jimmy Forsyth: 4, 13
WNLS / G. & D. Coates: 7
WNLS / Dept of Environmental Health:8

Published by
Newcastle Libraries & Information
Service
©City of Newcastle upon Tyne,
Education & Libraries Directorate,
Newcastle Libraries & Information
Service, 1993, reprinted 1998.

ISBN: 1 85795 011 9

In 1993 Westgate Road is the only major approach to Newcastle which has remained comparatively unchanged during this century. A West Central Route is now planned to cross the road at Blenheim Street and change is imminent; an ideal time to record the history of a road descending to the heart of old Newcastle. Today Westgate Road still follows the line chosen in AD 122 by Emperor Hadrian for the construction of a wall to mark the frontier of the Roman Empire. Newcastle was then Pons Aelius and the road stretched from this fort to the next fort at Condercum, Benwell. Westgate Road had the Wall as its foundations but little remains of Wall or Vallum until further west at Benwell and Denton.

This booklet describes Westgate Road as it is named today, tracing a promenade from its west boundary at the Venerable Bede Church down to the section past the end of Collingwood Street. Those of us who spent our youth in west Newcastle before the Second World War remember that the west part of the road and the adjoining West Road was still called the 'turnpike'. It was a popular promenade for local young people on a Sunday night, particularly between Brighton Grove and Two Ball Lonnen. Thomas Oliver's 1844 Plan of the Borough of Newcastle does not include Benwell and shows that the first part of our promenade went through Elswick Township (1841 pop. 2,384) named 'Turnpike Road'. In Westgate Township (pop. 10,063) Arthur Hill led to Cumberland Row then Westgate Hill. Finally through St John's Parish (pop. 8,741) we arrive in the ancient Westgate Street.

There was little change in the Elswick Township section until this century. Before that on the west boundary north of the road was North Elswick Hall, once occupied by Henry Milvain and now by the Sacred Heart School. South of the road was part of Richard Grainger's Elswick estate, purchased in 1839. Some of the large stone houses built there from 1865 still stand, such as 'Oakwood' no. 571. 'Wingrove House', once on the north side, was the home of the shipbuilder, John Wigham Richardson. Fenham Estates Co. bought Wingrove estate in 1898 but the name of the house lived on when streets were built from 1900 and Wingrove Tram Depot opened in 1904. The present General Hospital was also called the Wingrove between 1921 and 1930. Previously the name had been the Union Workhouse Hospital from 1870, thirty years after four Poor Houses moved to the site. The Nurses' Home opposite was built in 1928, next to Arthur's Hill Fire and Police Station which had stood from 1891. They were replaced in 1963.

The heavily populated Arthur's Hill suburb grew westward towards the hospital in the later 19th century mirroring the expansion of Armstrong's Works. Opposite Brighton Grove was a popular entertainment complex from 1911, the Brighton Cinema, Assembly Hall and Billiard Hall – from 1963 a bowling alley. The adjoining junction has seen horse trams, electric trams, trolley buses and petrol buses. The 1859 O.S. map shows little building between the hospital and Westgate Hill Cemetery (built 1829), a few Graingerville South houses, and the Elswick Mill on one side with Gloucester House and Prospect House (now a medical centre) on the north side. Gloucester House gave its name to a street almost opposite. The house was built by a Westgate Street tailor, Mr Laidler, who claimed royal patronage because he had repaired garments for the Duke of Gloucester. Locals called it 'Cabbage Hall' and in 1899 Westgate Hill School was built on the site. Westgate Road Baptist Church opened in 1886 after a new estate grew up nearby, west of Corporation Street, from the 1820s. It became called Arthur's Hill when Isaac Cookson built and named streets after his sons John, Edward and William: the estate was named after his eldest son Arthur. After 1961 it was demolished to make way for high rise flats.

The lower part of Westgate Road has been well documented and the remainder of our survey can be undertaken with the assistance of accompanying views and captions leading to the celebrated 'Lit and Phil' building housing the Society now celebrating its bicentenary.

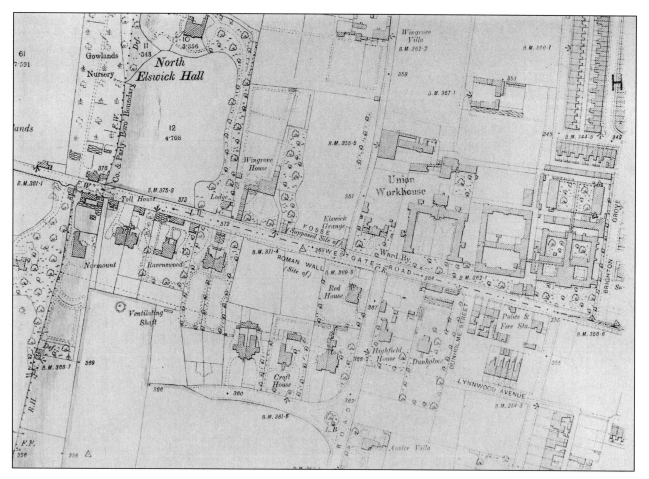

1. This 1894 plan shows the dotted boundary line, left, of Newcastle's west boundary from 1835 and of the present west end of Westgate Road. Bramble's Garage now stands on the site of the nearby Toll House. The Union Workhouse buildings are now part of the General Hospital.

2. Wingrove Tram Depot was opened in 1904 on what had been the grounds of shipbuilder John Wigham Richardson's Wingrove House. This photograph was said to have been taken at the opening but is probably from a later date. In 1993 car dealers Dutton-Forshaw use the adapted tram sheds as their Wingrove Depot.

3. A view across Westgate Road from Wingrove Avenue in the 1890s. Note the horse tram lines – carriers would need to water horses after the ascent from town. Red House, Grainger Park Road, was built c1880 and is now Church House, headquarters of the Newcastle Church of England Diocese.

4. 1963. On the right is the east corner of the 1928 Nurses' Home opposite the General Hospital. In the middle is the combined Arthur's Hill Police and Fire Station at the top of Dunholme Road, opened in 1891 and replaced in 1964.

5. A horse drawn tram, and the 1840 Union Workhouse, now the General Hospital, as seen from Bentinck Road in the 1890s. First World War reports mention 'Maconochie's' (on the side of the tram) as part of the rations for the troops. Note 'Elswick Lane', the old name for the road.

6. Electric trams started in 1901; in 1915 this tram stands near the hospital entrance. Graingerville North houses were built from the 1860s. Premises on the left were opened from 1911 as the Brighton Electric Theatre, Assembly and Billiard Halls. They became a bowling alley in 1963.

7. Headmaster T. Bowie, left, is proud of his 1936 scholarship winners. He achieved results by teaching by rote to obtain High School places for his Westgate Hill Council School 11 year olds. They pose wearing new uniforms for schools such as Dame Allan's, Rutherford and Newcastle Royal Grammar School. Before 1945 many would end up with different uniforms.

8. Nos. 340, 342 and 342½ Westgate Road in 1961, before land clearance opposite the cemetery for high rise flats. This was part of the first estate west of Corporation Street to be built, designated in the 1820s 'Arthur Hill' after the son of Isaac Cookson. The arch for horses, left, was to the Bell Street / West Street back lane.

9. 1920. Curved railings to deter body-snatchers guard Westgate Hill Non-Conformist Cemetery (built 1829) with St Matthew's Church behind. On the left of this view are the ends of John and Tindal Streets, the Plague burial ground, and the clock tower of Westgate Hall Methodist Mission (1903-1973).

10. Looking down Westgate Hill to Westgate in 1830. Some of the terraced houses on the left were once called Cumberland Row. The quiet quadrangle of Summerhill lay behind the houses right. The Castle Keep, and the churches, left to right, of All Saints, St Nicholas, and St John, are prominent.

SPOT CASH

MARQUIS of BLANDFO

WINE & SP

ASKWITHS ASKWITHS'

DRESS
MANTLE MAKE

PERTH
DYE
WORKS

MILLINERS

H & G PYE

FUNERAL OF THE LATE BISHOP OF NEWCASTLE JUNE 3 1907

11. The funeral procession of Arthur Thomas Lloyd, Bishop of Newcastle, passes the end of Blandford Street on June 3rd 1907. Benwell Towers was then the Bishop's residence. Note the Marquis of Blandford pub, 173 Westgate Road, and its connection with nearby street names, Blenheim, Churchill, Duke, as well as Marlborough Crescent.

12. Looking up the hill from Blenheim Street c1910. The outline of Westgate Hall Methodist Mission is just visible at the top. Newton & Co., nos. 159-167, were machine factors. Early in the century the large houses right became occupied by practices of doctors and dentists, as apartment houses or for small businesses and voluntary organisations.

13. This 1956 view of the corner of Westgate Road and Blenheim Street is due to change after 1993 to make way for the West Central Route. Hoardings now cover the Carlisle Hotel and Sinclair's Tobacco building now contains flats. Alongside the latter a narrow lane leads to Temple Street, once the venue of Newcastle's first synagogue, built 1838.

14. A 1914 view of the Salvation Army City Temple entrance, left, and the Pavilion, right. The latter closed as a cinema in 1975 and was demolished in 1992. Past the Pavilion was another cinema, the Stoll (1919-1974) which had opened in 1867 as the Tyne Theatre and has now reverted to that name.

15. The West Gate in the Town Walls once stood here. In 1884-6 this is a view from Cross Street across Westgate Road to no. 91, Lockhart's Cocoa Rooms and the entrance to Pink Lane, right. The latter led to the Pink Tower of the Town Wall, and was part of the Pomerium giving defenders within the Wall access to it.

16. A 1789 illustration of the strongly fortified West Gate. The Town Walls were built from the 13th century and this gate was demolished 1805-1811. The town's 15th century 'Dick Whittington', Roger Thornton, was celebrated in the rhyme, "At the West-Gate came Thornton in, With a hap, and a half-penny, and a lamb's skin."

17. The wedge-shaped Cross House at the corner of Westgate Road, left, and Fenkle Street, caught fire at 4.00 p.m. on December 23rd, 1919, when celluloid ciné film ignited in the basement. Firemen's ladders were too short and ten people died; office workers jumped into sheets. Nearby is the Joseph Cowen (the younger) monument, erected after his death in 1900.

To the MEMBERS of the SUBSCRIPTION ROOMS in NEWCASTLE upon TYNE This View of the ASSEMBLY HOUSE, &c. in that Town, Engraved at their Expence is respectfully Inscribed by their very obliged & obedt. humble Servt. John S.

18. The Assembly Rooms were built in Westgate Street 1774-6, in "The pleasantest part of the town inhabited by the clergy and gentry". The Rooms were paid for by public subscription, used for balls and dinners, and London newspapers were in the newsroom on the day of publication. Since 1981 elegant listed buildings on the right have been restored by Newcastle Arts Centre.

19. The '850 Years Appeal' for the church dedicated to St John the Baptist is underway in 1993. In this 1905 photograph the Trustee Savings Bank is on the left. Church and Bank were separated by muddy St John's Lane until Grainger Street was extended from the Bigg Market in 1868, bringing the pavement up to the church.

STEPHENSON'S MONUMENT. NEWCASTLE-ON-TYNE.

20. This view of c1910 includes the Union Club, right, built 1874 but today long unoccupied. Local sculptor John Lough was responsible for the George Stephenson monument erected 1862. The area was once the West 'Spital, site of the 12th century St Mary the Virgin Hospital and later the Royal Grammar School. The Express Inn façade represents the site's historic associations.

21. c1900. Westgate Road, behind Stephenson's monument, crosses past the end of Collingwood Street, centre, and continues behind the Victorian Gothic Neville Hall, right. The Mining Institute and the 'Lit and Phil' are part of the Neville Hall group of buildings which were erected from 1822, and are of inestimable value to our heritage.